# Gaudí

## The entire works

Text
**Joan Bassegoda i Nonell**
(Reial Càtedra Gaudí)

Photographs
**Pere Vivas | Ricard Pla**

TRIANGLE ▼ POSTALS

# Gaudí

# 5

# Gaudí's secret

Joan Bassegoda i Nonell

Much has been written about Gaudí's unique architecture from historical, critical and technical-constructive perspectives. There have also been attempts at biography, despite the few reliable facts that are available regarding his life. We have even seen published, in the interests of mythomania, esoteric, mysterious or fantasy-filled interpretations of the supposed symbols contained in the master architect's work.

Gaudí is the architect of simplicity, the author of works that are governed by a continuous and logical sense of rationality and functionalism. Unfortunately, simple is generally understood in architectural terms as that which has been drawn with a compass and set square based on an elementary Euclidian geometry. For centuries this geometry has ruled architectural forms, forming regular polyhedrons, spheres or ellipsoids which are simple to draw but which do not have to be either rational or functional.

The geometry of architects, from the Pharaonic pyramids to the glass in the courtyard of the Louvre, has always been the same; abstract geometry, which means using forms that are rarely produced in nature, but which are easy to draw with the compass and set square.

This geometry is the result of a mental process of simplification, thinking about the easiness of the plan and not the final objective of the architecture, which is the comfort of those who use it.

It is said that Father Enric d'Ossó — today Saint Enric d'Ossó— asked Gaudí in 1888 to explain to him what the Theresan College would be like, under construction at the time. Gaudí answered with a truly categorical phrase: *It will be good in this house.* This expression contains the deepest knowledge of architecture. Houses are built to feel good inside them, not so that the architect wins international prizes or that the building is listed as a monument or artistic and historic site. Such accessories are also possible in a building where one feels good, but they are neither necessary nor sufficient.

Gaudí, son of the light-filled Camp de Tarragona county, gifted with an exceptional spirit of observation and an almost child-like naivety, was able to realise that nature is capable of creating forms of great beauty and usefulness, forms that survive, are repeated and which give generation after generation of people a great deal of pleasure.

Totally logical forms and structures, the only ones possible, are adapted to each case and circumstance and always pleasant and attractive for the living beings of the Earth, whether human or animal.

All in all, these natural structures are almost never formed with the abstract geometry of architects, but by means of another, called ruled geometry, of warped surfaces formed by straight lines. Many natural structures are made up of fibres: wood is fibrous, as are bones and muscles; fibres not over a planc, but in space, arranged in the four possible forms of ruled geometry.

Gaudí, a keen observer, noticed this and all his architecture was based on the idea of transferring ruled geometry to architectural construction. He was the first to build vaults of hyperbolic paraboloids, one of the ruled surfaces, in the portico of the crypt of the Colònia Güell in Santa Coloma de Cervelló —. He was the first architect to do so, since nature had arranged them since time immemorial on the leaves of trees, the tendons between our fingers or in the passes between two mountains.

The concept of rationality in Gaudí's architecture may seem like a contradiction in terms when viewing his buildings, which appear more Baroque than anything else, but this apparent contradiction comes from assuming that rationality is focussed only on the use of simple geometry, whereas the irrational would be left for Baroque forms, presumably fanciful.

In the 18th century the Franciscan Carlo Lodoli criticised over-elaborate Baroque façades and argued that the outside of the building must correspond to its interior arrangement. He proposed that furniture should be adapted to the shapes of the human body and praised the solution of Vene-

**Adornment on the ceiling of La Pedrera**

tian gondolas, where each part is made to fulfil its specific task.

Modern criticism has seen the thoughts of Lodoli as the beginning of rationalism, of so-called functionalism, in short, the modern movement.

However, a big mistake is made here. Gaudí designed buildings where the façade is only the external translation of the interior layout, as is the case of the La Pedrera where from the different floors one has the sensation of being outside the house. He designed the furnishing in the Casas Calvet, Batl-ló— and Milà in totally anatomic forms, adapted perfectly to the human body and stated that if he had not been an architect he would have liked to have been a boat builder, boats being made up of forms adapted perfectly to the aquatic environment in which they must move around.

He shared, unknowingly, the opinion of Vincenzo Danti who in 1567 stated that the most beautiful flower is that which best fulfils the objectives that nature itself sets it. Gaudí argued that flowers have bright colours and pleasant perfumes, not to inspire poets and painters, but to attract insects and facilitate reproduction of the species.

Functionality does not consist of using simple forms, traceable with compass and set square, the compass is in the eyes said Michelangelo, but in taking those which the wisdom of nature generously offers, although with another type of geometry.

An obvious case is Gaudí's constant use of the catenary arch, which is one that takes on the form of a chain hung from its ends. This arch is the best mechanically, the one that works best, but has not been often used by architects because it is difficult to draw with the compass. For Gaudí if it was the most mechanical, it had to be the most beautiful.

Gaudí thought seeking out functionality led to finding beauty whereas seeking out beauty directly led one to come up against aesthetics, the theory of art and other abstract and philosophical concepts that bothered his simple mentality.

One of his most significant statements compiled by his scholars is that creation continues through the involvement of men, since it is not men that create, but through investigation discover the laws of nature and with them continue the work of the Creator. It does not involve inventing anything new, but rather studying what already exists and trying to improve on it.

Gaudí clearly applied this theory in his way of interpreting Gothic style. In 1771 the Frenchman Jacques François Blondel said that the Gothic vault is identified with the origin of natural art on being an imitation of a tree with its trunk as the column and the branches extended as the ribs of the vaults. Gaudí considered Gothic as the most structural of historical styles. As far as he was concerned, the architects of the Renaissance were simple decorators, but the Gothic solutions with pointed arches and flying buttresses were imperfect. He proposed and produced the perfecting of Gothic with the catenary arches and inclined columns.

Gaudí expressed the most outstanding case of structural rationalism with the famous model for calculating the structure of the church of the Colònia Güell. By means of a series of cords and strings hanging from the ceiling of a small room alongside the works, he achieved, by hanging small canvas bags containing pellets from the cords, with a weight proportional to the loads that the structure would have to withstand, a form that, photographed and reversing the image, gave the exact arrangement of pillars, arches and vaults, without any possibility of error, since the determination of the forms obeyed solely the law of gravity. We could say that Isaac Newton, who discovered the law of gravity, collaborated with Gaudí on this project.

It is admirable to come up with a rigorously exact calculation without a single mathematical operation. This was the opinion of the teacher, architect and engineer Fèlix Cardellach who in 1910 said of Gaudí that he had such a flow of constructive ideas in his mind that the laws of nature, instead of standing in his way, are for him an instrument and toy of progress. The simple freedom with which he moves within his works could be defined as the emancipation of all doctrines, with the prevailing one being reason.

Gaudí's architecture is alive and palpitating. J. F. Ràfols, Gaudí's first biographer, said that for the Greeks the life of architecture arose from, without wanting to, the façade, whereas Gaudí worked on his search as if he sunk his hands and fists into the very heart of the soul of the static part in order to squeeze the juice of life from the core. Referring to the Casa Milà, the abovementioned author adds, a work that would have no equal around the world, that it submerges the artistic conception in the sea of life and gives it that feeling that confuses the brain and inflames the aesthetic thrill in the heart.

Gaudí was lucky enough to meet and work with Mr. Eusebi Güell, his real friend and patron, for whom over a period of 40 years, from 1878 to 1918, he produced the most important works, apart from the Sagrada Família.

The architect was able to freely develop his constructive personality although the basic ideas actually came from Güell, or from his collaborators such as Verdaguer or Picó i Campamar. A man of the *Renaixença* movement, Güell loved Greek mythology, and wanted to recreate the Garden of the Hesperides on the Güell Estate in Les Corts de Sarrià, in the palace in Carrer Nou de la Rambla, in the wine cellars of the Garraf or in Park Güell, turned into the new city of Delphos. Gaudí was subjected to the concepts and symbols his client desired, but he produced his own art and the result is truly spectacular.

On the other hand the Franciscan concept of love of nature turned him into a deeply religious person. He was brought up in the heart of a Christian artisan family, having studied in the Esculapian school. After experiencing the revolutionary excitement of 1868 in Reus, from his knowledge and almost immediate abandonment of anarchist or socialist ideas, in some ways present in the Matazonesa Cooperative which he worked for in his formative years, he led a life quite distinct from that of the famous architects of his time. He lived in the old quarter and in the Eixample district and later living in the show house of Park Güell from 1906 and from there he walked every day to the Sagrada Família and the other works in progress. From 1911, he devoted himself exclusiverely to the temple, where he lived the last year of his life.

He frequented the cathedral and church of Sant Felip Neri, where his spiritual guide was, was a member of the Cercle Artístic de Sant Lluc, a meeting place for catholic artists and was friends with members of the clergy as important as the bishops Torras i Bages of Vic, Campins of Mallorca and Grau of Astorga, as well as priests such as Verdaguer, Casanovas or Collell.

He dedicated his time to architectural work and never took time to write, travel, give talks or have a social life. He never married and friends were his collaborators on works, particularly Lorenç Matamala, Josep and Lluís Badia, Francesc Berenguer, Joan Rubió, Josep Maria Jujol or Domènec Sugrañes.

His sense of logic made him conceive methods for the art of construction in such a way that many construction workers not working on the Sagrada Família site came along to observe the work of their colleagues.

Beneath a rather stern, but truly good-natured appearance, he hid an extreme sensitivity and on several occasions suffered depressive moments, which he fought with rests in Vic in 1910 and Puigcerdà in 1911.

His library was extremely small and he said that the best book on architecture was the tree which he could see through the window of his studio.

He saw himself as a child of the Mediterranean, where art is possible and finds its maximum expression; he considered his home county, Camp de Tarragona, as a typical spot of the basin of Mare Nostrum and Barcelona, the city where he lived for 57 years, the plot of land for the greater part of his work and especially the temple of the Sagrada

Família, where he threw in all his creative power with the demonstration of the real existence of a naturalist architecture based on ruled geometry and in the spirit of the Catholic religion, which sank deeply into his believer's soul.

The presence of Christian symbols in all his buildings, including those that were not of a religious nature, clearly shows this. He was extremely upset when he was stopped from crowning La Pedrera with the gilded bronze image standing 4.5 metres high that should have represented the Blessed Virgin with Saint Gabriel and Saint Michael.

In the words of the Chinese architect Hou Teh-Chien, Gaudí is a philosopher who expresses his ideas through his buildings. Gaudí's architecture is a metaphor of nature, a totally rational constructive version of the structures and forms of the three kingdoms, vegetable, animal and mineral, that make up the world.

Gaudí's architecture is timeless since it does not rely on styles or tendencies, and still gives pleasure three-quarters of a century after his death in the same way as flowers or mountains do.

Children and the uninitiated understand and feel his architecture better than actual architects since it penetrates directly into the souls of people and does not require the explanations of critics or historians.

He was a contemporary of artistic movements such as eclecticism, Catalan modernism, *noucentisme* or rationalism, but it is impossible to classify it as representative of any of them.

He left the door open to a way of building closer to nature, more balanced and ecological. His message to the generations that followed does not consist of asking for his forms to be imitated, but that nature's forms are studied so that multiple, diverse and useful solutions can be found.

The path taken by Gaudí, however, as he said himself, was self-sacrificing and, at times, painful, since in order to obtain the best results you have to work hard and make a lot of mistakes.

Inspiration consists of doing apparently easy things that in reality require continuous efforts.

You have to look for Gaudí's secret in his way of being both simple and demanding at the same time. He was lucky enough not to have any forbears who were architects and therefore did not suffer the professional habits or corruptions of those born with the training of the age-old artistic science of architecture.

He strongly appreciated popular architecture, that which is produced without architects, or projects or calculus, but with the material at hand and with simply utilitarian intentions.

His is the architecture of natural reality that is presented as if it were the result of an illusion. It resembles the creation of a fairy tale and in contrast fits the more permanent truth based on the immutable laws of the world.

# Other places

② **El Capricho**
⑥ **Episcopal Palace of Astorga**
⑦ **Casa Botines**
⑫ **Cathedral of Mallorca**

# Barcelona

① **Casa Vicens**
③ **Güell Pavilions**
④ **Palau Güell**
⑤ **Theresan College**
⑨ **Casa Calvet**
⑩ **Bellesguard Tower**
⑪ **Park Güell**
⑬ **Casa Batlló**
⑭ **La Pedrera**
⑯ **Temple of the Sagrada Família**

② Comillas

⑦ León

⑥ Astorga

• Barcelona

⑫ Palma de Mallorca

⑧ **Güell Bodegas**
⑮ **Crypt of the Colònia Güell**

• La Pobla de Lillet

Santa Coloma de Cervelló

⑮

Sitges

⑧

● **Barcelona**

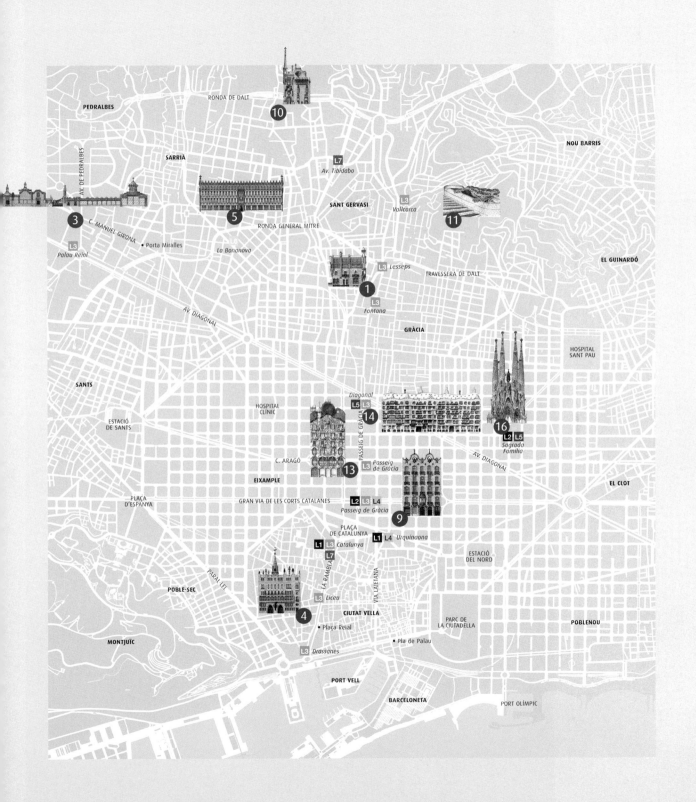

PEDRALBES

NOU BARRIS

SARRIÀ

**L7**
Av. Tibidabo

SANT GERVASI

**L3**
Vallcarca

10

RONDA DE DALT

**3**

C. MANUEL GIRONA

**L3**
Palau Reial

• Porta Miralles

La Bonanova

RONDA GENERAL MITRE

5

EL GUINARDÓ

**L3**
Lesseps

TRAVESSERA DE DALT

1

**L3**
Fontana

AV. DIAGONAL

GRÀCIA

HOSPITAL
SANT PAU

11

SANTS

ESTACIÓ
DE SANTS

HOSPITAL
CLÍNIC

Diagonal
**L5** **L3**

14

16

**L2** **L5**
Sagrada
Família

AV. DIAGONAL

EL CLOT

PLAÇA
D'ESPANYA

C. ARAGÓ

EIXAMPLE

13

**L3**
Passeig
de Gràcia

GRAN VIA DE LES CORTS CATALANES

**L2** **L3** **L4**
Passeig de Gràcia

9

**L1** **L4** Urquinaona

ESTACIÓ
DEL NORD

PLAÇA
DE CATALUNYA

**L1** **L3** Catalunya
**L7**

POBLE-SEC

PARAL·LEL

**L3** Liceu

4

CIUTAT VELLA

• Plaça Reial

PARC DE
LA CIUTADELLA

POBLENOU

MONTJUÏC

**L3** Drassanes

• Pla de Palau

PORT VELL

BARCELONETA

PORT OLÍMPIC

1

2

# Early works Barcelona

On the walls of the aquarium situated behind the waterfall of the Parc de la Ciutadella, the work of Josep Fontserè Mestres in 1875, according to Josep F. Ràfols Fontanals in his 1929 biography of Gaudí, the circular relief work representing a lizard between leaves of aquatic plants would be the work of the young Gaudí, still a student, under the orders of the head of works of the park.

In 1883 Father Jacint Verdaguer asked his friend, the Canon of Vic Jaume Collell i Bancells, for a Latin text to place in a fountain that Gaudí had planned in the gardens of the Casa Güell, today the Royal Palace of Pedralbes. Gaudí had dedicated the fountain to Hercules, who appeared at the top of a pedestal, wearing the helmet he made from the head of the lion of Nemea. The sole spout of the fountain has the form of a dragon, which could well be Ladon, the protector of the garden of the Hesperides who was killed by Hercules with a single shot.

According to an official of Barcelona City Council, in June 1878, Gaudí presented the project for some lampposts. Gaudí designed two models, one with three arms and another with six, which were finally placed in the Pla de Palau and the Plaça Reial, respectively.

3

Plaça Reial                    Pla de Palau

# ❶ Casa Vicens Barcelona

Casa Vicens is in Carrer Carolines. The main façade had a gallery (now modified) that was closed by some large hinged wooden shutters, and in the centre was placed an old Renaissance basin with a type of metallic spider's web, over which the water splashed and, with the sun, divided up into the colours of the rainbow. Opposite this façade he built the waterfall that was demolished in 1946.

The inside of the house is like a fairy tale, the ceilings are of small wooden polychromed beams adorned with floral themes as well as polychromes in papier maché. There is a smoking room with a level ceiling of mocárabe designs that recall the Generalife of Granada.

The system of the two-panelled doors that open simultaneously is quite brilliant, and also of note are the chimneys and details of the floors and walls. On the first floor are the sgraffito walls reproducing reeds, rose trees and other plants that could be found by the neighbouring Cassoles or En Malla streams.

On the corners he placed some projecting galleries that the master builder did not have much faith in; he waited several hours after completing the work expecting them to fall down.

Casa Vicens also contains other decorative details that show Gaudí's sensitivity, an example of which is his decision to place a ceramic bird hanging from an invisible thread over the dining room fireplace and which, with the hot air, balanced as if it were flying in that unreal atmosphere of cherry tree branches on the ceiling and climbing ivies over a gilded background on the walls.

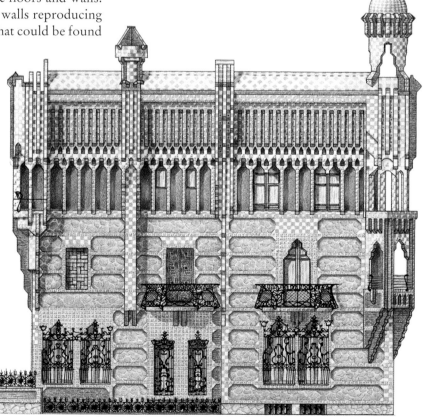

1 *Fumoir* of Arab inspiration

2 Glazed tiles on
  the façade with floral
  motifs
3 Iron grille inspired
  by the European
  palms of the garden
4 General view

2

3

5    6

# ② El Capricho Comillas

In 1883, Gaudí was given the commission by Mr Máximo Díaz de Quijano to undertake a project for a holiday retreat beside the Marquis of Comillas' Sobrellano Palace, in the selfsame town in Cantabria. The Capricho building, a strict contemporary of Casa Vicens, is yet another example of the plenitude of this oriental tendency in which Gaudí found such prodigious solutions.

El Capricho is a building with a lower ground floor, ground floor and attic. The ground floor is lengthened and has a side entrance with a set of four columns that support the tower, reminding one of a Persian minaret. On the culmination of the tower, all of it rendered with the same ceramics that he used on the terrace of Casa Vicens, there is a delightful lantern supported by four cast iron columns and an elegant veranda. The similarity is also apparent in the capitals of the entrance columns, which are a repetition of the European palm of the grille in the Barcelona house, over which are placed several birds. The large dining room-lounge takes on all the height of the building and has a large window with sash windows, which on the counterweights have tubular bells, each with a different tone, so that they make a lovely sound when opening and closing them.

The house was later enlarged with a rear section which disfigured it, and its Arab tiling was replaced by fibre-cement, but is still conserves the vision of the whole within the park, all of it a deep green. The angular balconies are skilfully attained, and their handrails form a bench so that people can sit on them facing the building with their backs to the path.

It is reputed that Gaudí was never in Comillas, although this is difficult to believe when looking at the meticulousness of the detail and the perfection of the finishes. In any case, the construction was directed on site by Cristobal Cascante, an assistant to Gaudí.

The chimneys crowning the roofing of El Capricho are also extremely personal and underline this unusual path that Gaudí followed throughout his life work, designed not only to channel the smoke, but also as really interesting decorative elements.

In early 1977 "El Capricho" was bought by a family that had it beautifully restored and today it is a restaurant.

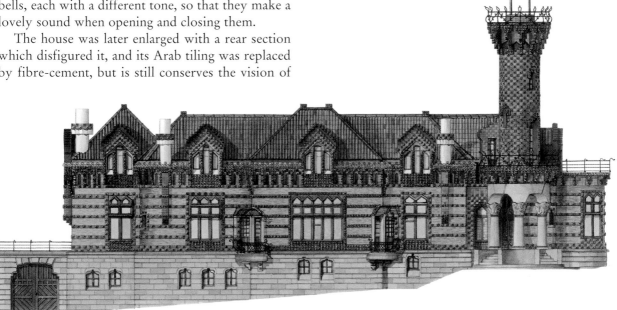

1 **Ceramic covering of sunflowers**

Estate of the Sobrellano Palace, Comillas. Cantabria

2 **Balcony-bench**
3 **Entrance porch**
4 **General view**

2

3

1 Anagram of Güell on the floor of the stables

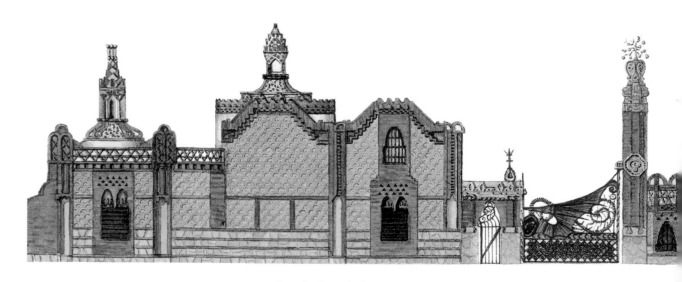

# ③ **Pavilions of the Güell Estate** Barcelona

Around 1884 Mr Eusebi Güell entrusted Gaudí with some building work on the Les Corts de Sarrià estate, to reform the house already standing and to build the enclosure wall and the porter's lodge pavilions. On this task Gaudí threw himself whole-heartedly into the best of his orientalist period.

Gaudí surrounded the whole estate with a masonry wall, in which he placed several doorways. The main entrance was closed off with a gate that was built in 1885 in the Vallet y Piqué workshop. It represents a menacing chained and very big dragon with glass eyes. On either side of the gate were the stables, exercising ring and porter's lodge. The former is covered with bricked vaulting with a catenary outline that is supported on other catenary arches. This form, which he had used in Mataró and in Casa Vicens, found its greatest expression in the Güell estate. The exercising ring is covered with a cupola of an approximate hyperboloid form, in the upper part of which there is a spacious lantern. The porter's lodge is also covered with three cupolas crowned with some vents in the form of chimneys covered with ceramic fragments.

The two entrance pavilions, facing Avinguda de Pedralbes, were restored between 1967 and 1977 for the headquarters of the Real Càtedra Gaudí. The restoration has given back the building all its freshness and intention of Gaudí's early period, and even though it represents an emphatic oriental treatment of the brickwork and stucco of the exteriors, the inside is a wonder of really modern forms launched into the air with an infinite sense of elegance.

Güell's father-in-law, Antonio López, Marquis of Comillas (1817-1883), spent long periods in the Güell Estate, and was the patron of the poet Father Jacint Verdaguer who dedicated his poem "L'Atlàntida" to him. This epic poem tells of the eleventh labour that Eurystheus, King of Mycenae, set Hercules, making him steal some oranges from the garden of the Hesperides, guarded by a fierce dragon called Ladon and three maidens, the Hesperides. When the Marquis of Comillas died in 1883, Güell, using the poetry of Verdaguer and the art of Gaudí, decided to pay him a very special homage by turning the whole area of the Güell Estate into a new garden of the Hesperides. To do this he put the wrought iron gate at the entrance fixed to a pillar, the top of which has an orange tree made of antimony. He had elms, black poplar and willow trees planted in the garden, corresponding to the trees that the Hesperides were turned into for not taking care of guarding the oranges. Thus the homage to the Marquis of Comillas acquired both poetic and mythological aspects.

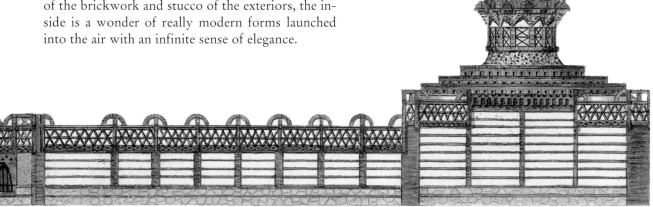

2

3

4

5

6

7

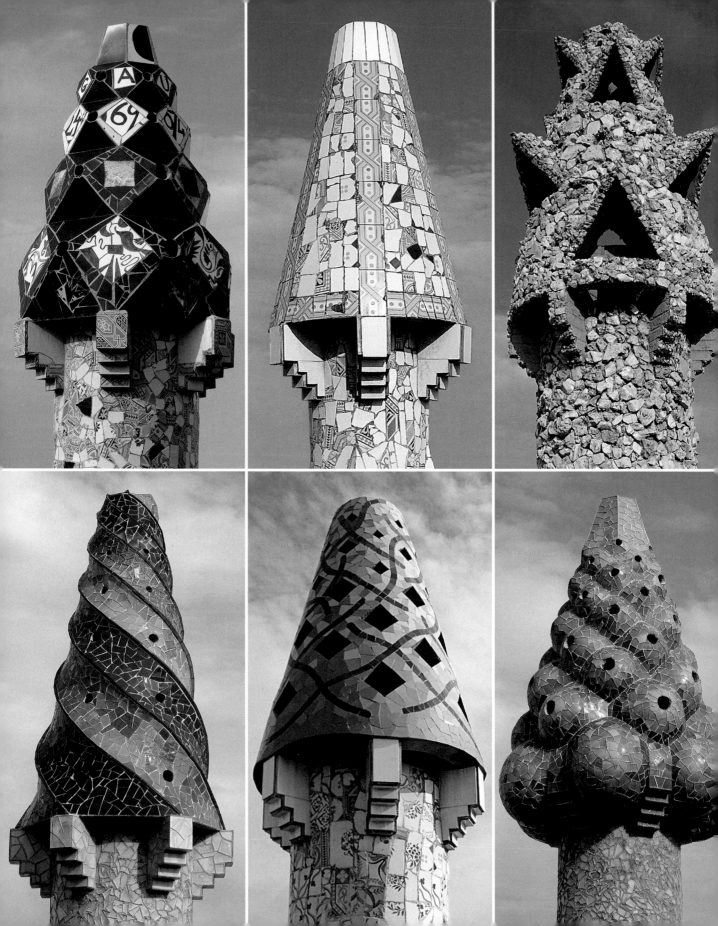

# ❹ **Palau Güell** Barcelona

It was built between 1886 and 1888. The constructive solutions provided by Gaudí are as varied as they are unique. In the basement, totally built with brickwork mushroom-shaped columns and bricked vaulting, the stables were installed with a series of vents in the form of chimneys that carried the unpleasant smells up to the flat roof. The low part of the building was made with stone from Eusebio's quarries on the Garraf coast.

The entrance to the hallway consists of two gateways in the form of closed catenary arches with wrought iron grilles between which there is a coat of arms of Catalonia in three-dimensional wrought iron. Above is a mezzanine where the owner's office was with polished stone walls and flooring and iron joists and main beams. On the main floor the ceilings are made of jointed cypress and eucalyptus wood, the ceiling being both decorative and load bearing.

The street façade is made up of three successive areas of which the central one leads to the grand hall which takes on the whole height of the building, and which also served as a chapel, and is covered with a revolving paraboloid cupola with a series of holes in a starred form that enables the outside light to pass through small windows in the upper conical structure. The family bedrooms are on the top floors and higher up those of the servants with metal and wood decorations which anticipate the solutions that the Modernist architects used later.

The flat roof is quite spectacular with the conical form that crowns the hall and the twenty chimneys and vents, the kitchen and service ones in brick and the others of broken ceramic, all in different geometrical forms with intersections of cones, helicoids, spheres or pyramids.

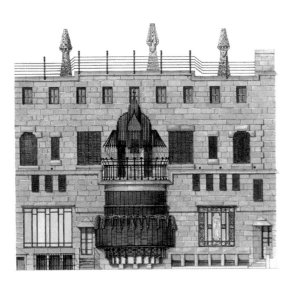

1 **Chimneys**

2 **Catenary arch and
coat of arms
at the entrance**
3 **Stables**
4 **Bedroom capital**

4

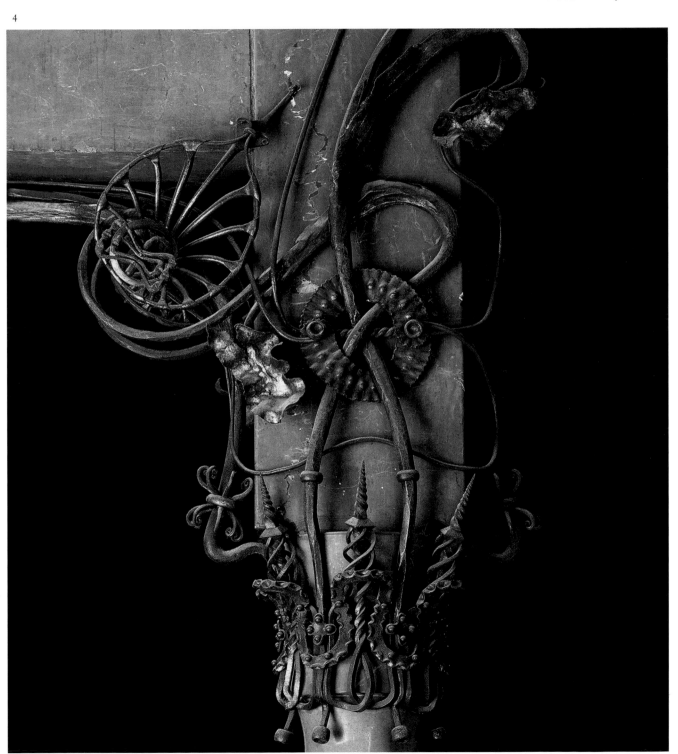

5

5 **Cupola of the main hall**
6 **Flat roof**

6

# ⑤ **Theresan College** Barcelona

Enric d'Ossó founded the Congregation of Theresan Nuns. In 1887 he began the construction of the building, using the project of the architect Joan B. Pons Trabal (1855-1927), but very shortly after Father Ossó, well aware of Gaudí's fame and religiousness, passed on to him the job of finishing the college, situated in Carrer Ganduxer.

In 1888, Gaudí took over the direction of the works and began a building of highly original forms. He made the walls in masonry with layers of open brickwork, just like in Casa Vicens, with very long windows and false catenary arches. The whole building, of rectangular ground plan, is crowned with elegant crenellations. The sober exterior appearance must have obeyed the desire for poverty and the lack of means of Father Ossó, but Gaudí also stamped the building with an aspect of a solid fortress, as a symbol of the mystical dwellings of the saint from Avila.

One of the most daring conceptions of Gaudí's structural ideas can be seen in the first floor of the collage, designed as an indoor cloister with a series of light walls that are supported on the keystones of a series of thin catenary arches that rest over very slender columns, made up of a single row of 10 mm bricks called *picholines*. These arches and their thin columns make up a structured area with a charming effect.

On the ground floor some large corbels support the weight of the slender columns of the floor above and pass them on to some solid open brickwork pillars.

The decoration, based on open brickwork and glazed tiling on the façade, forms a joyous decorative detail alongside the severity of the masonry walls. In the corners some pinnacles appear with the four-armed cross, so beloved by Gaudí.

Also of note here are the bold grilles, both of the windows and the main doorway.

Regarding this building, Gaudí said something well worth remembering ad lapidem. Father Ossó asked Gaudí, "What will the building be like when it is finished?" "It will be fine in this house", replied Gaudí giving a superb lesson in the best architecture.

1 **Arches of the cloister**

# ⑥ **Episcopal Palace** Astorga

Joan Baptista Grau Vallespinós was appointed Bishop of Astorga in 1886, in the province of León, after having been Vicar-General of the Archdiocese of Tarragona for some years. Shortly after taking possession of the mitre of Astorga the Episcopal palace burnt down and the newly-appointed bishop entrusted his fellow citizen of the Tarragona region, Gaudí, with the project for the new palace and residence.

Gaudí made studies of the nature of the climate and the actual site of Astorga and in 1887 signed a full project that was presented to the Ministry of Pardon and Justice which had to finance the work. The process for obtaining the works licence was delayed for two years and it was not until 24 June 1889 that the first stone of the new palace was laid. Its construction progressed relatively slowly and in 1893, shortly before Bishop Grau died, Gaudí renounced the directorship of the works due to disagreements with the Cathedral Chapter. The building was not completed until 1915 and the third floor and roofing is not the work of Gaudí, but of Ricardo García Guereta.

The architect gave an interpretation of Gothic style using Bierzo granite on the outside walls and brick vaulting in the interior with glazed ceramic ribs produced in the neighbouring town of Jiménez de Jamuz. The palace has a lower ground floor surrounded by a moat for storerooms and stables, the ground floor being for reception and offices and the main floor with the bishop's residence, the throne room, the special events dining room, law office and chapel, all of them rooms with large windows and ample spaces.

The palace was never inhabited by bishops and today houses the Museum of the Pilgrims' Ways with items from the Roman way of Asturica in the basement and objects from the medieval Saint James Way on the main floor.

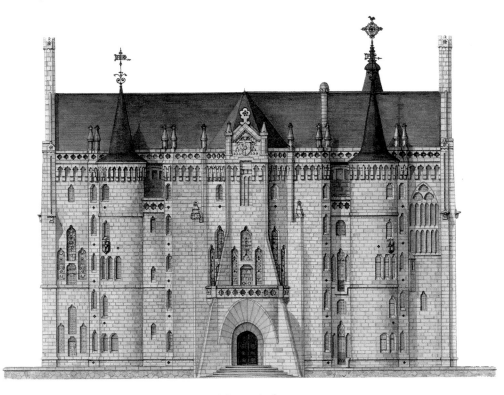

1 **Ribbed vault**

2  General view

3  One of the three
   zinc angels with the
   Episcopal insignia that
   should have crowned
   the building

2   3

4

5

4 **Ribs of the vault**
5 **Columns and vaults in the basement**
6 **Ceramic covering**

6

# ⑦ **Casa Botines** León

At the same time as the Episcopal Palace of Astorga was being built, Gaudí received the commission for the project for a house to let in the Plaza de San Marcelo in León for Messrs. Fernández and Andrés who had a textile business inherited from Juan Homs Botinàs. The house was called Botines (1891-1892) due to the deformation of the surname of the Catalan trader established in León.

This detached building is made up of the store-room basement, also surrounded by a ditch, ground floor as the shop and three floors more, the first or main floor being two homes for the owners and the others with four homes on each floor to be rented out. The outside is of limestone along toned-down Gothic lines, with cylindrical towers in the corners and a slate roof over wooden frameworks. The homes were extremely comfortable and well ventilated and lit via the façades and the courtyards separated by wooden walls.

In Gaudí's absence, the works were led by Claudi Alsina, who placed the only sculpture of the house over the front door. It is the work of Antoni Cantó and Llorenç Matamala and represents Saint George fighting against the dragon.

It is interesting to note that the structure of the house is made up of cast iron pillars, iron joists and main beams without other load walls than the exterior ones: in other words, totally free open floors. The building was acquired in 1931 by the Caja de Ahorros y Monte de Piedad de León (Savings Bank) and later passed into the ownership o Caja España, which between 1994 and 1996 restored it and is today a cultural centre.

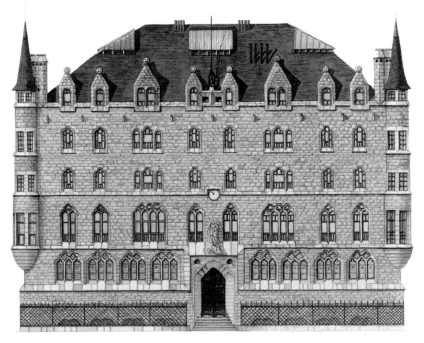

1 **Saint George over the main entrance**

Plaza de San Marcelo, León

2

3

4

5

# ⑧ Güell Bodegas Sitges

His palace completed, Eusebi Güell entrusted Gaudí with the construction of a building for the Güell Bodegas, on the Garraf coast, south of Barcelona. It is a rocky, wild area overlooking the Mediterranean Sea where there had been a building used as a bodega, which was owned by the Cathedral Chapter of Barcelona.

Between 1895 and 1898 Gaudí, with the help of Francesc Berenguer Mestres (1866-1914), his faithful collaborator since 1883, built a construction of several floors over the underground bodegas. The new building has a triangular elevation and housed new bodegas, homes and, on the top floor, a chapel.

It is covered outside with local stone so it blends in perfectly with the surrounding landscape. At the end of the top floor, in front of the chapel is an open viewpoint supported by thin inclining columns following the outline of the acute angle of the roof. The interior arches and vaults are catenary and the whole piece produces a great sensation of balance and solidity.

Güell also used the building as a hunting pavilion for himself and his friends. The chapel has a stone altar and wrought iron candelabras and crucifix and above it there is a stone steeple with a bell called "Isabel" in homage to Mrs. Güell and the date 1897. There is a very schematic plan with Gaudí's signature and the date 1895 which is preserved in the municipal archives in Sitges, the town that the Garraf property or estate forms part of. Next to the road is the entrance with an original wrought iron grille and the porter's stone and brick home, in amusing forms.

1 **Main entrance**

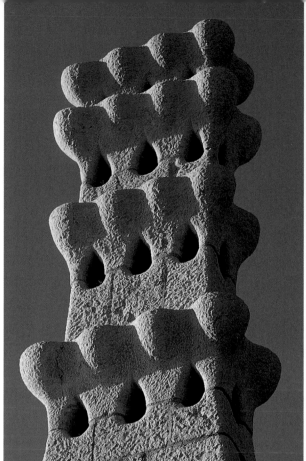

2

3

4

5

# ⑨ Casa Calvet Barcelona

In Carrer Casp in Barcelona, Gaudí built a house of flats between party walls for the textile manufacturer Pere Màrtir Calvet. The building has a façade facing the street made entirely of sandstone from Montjuïc, with balconies of flagstones sculpted with numerous items of relief work and a complex gallery on the first floor with relief work that represents mushrooms, since the owner was a mycologist and, at the top the horn of Amalthea overflowing with fruit.

Over the central door is the letter "C" of Calvet in relief and a cypress tree as a symbol of hospitality. The lift is placed in the stairwell and has an extraordinary cabin of carved wood and wrought iron, which is a work of art in itself. On the ground floor the landing of the stairway is supported on Solomonic columns of artificial granite and the walls are painted with representations of vines with bunches of grapes and the slogan of the poetry competition, the Jocs Florals, "Faith, Fatherland and Love".

At the top of the street-facing façade there are some curved crowning pieces on the upper part of which are stone spheres with some wrought iron crosses. Further down are three sculpted heads, that of Saint Peter Martyr and those of Saint Genesius the notary and Saint Genesius the actor, in recognition of the owner's birthplace, Sant Genís de Vilassar and its patron saints.

Just as Gaudí himself stated, the building is inspired by Catalan Baroque, although the organic and naturalist spirit is added, characteristic of the works in Gaudí's final stage.

Of great interest inside the house is the wooden furniture, both of the office and the owner's home. In the office there is screen with the different windows to attend to the customers. This oak screen is totally sculpted to the rouge and, on the outer part, in the customer's view, there are two-fronted benches, also in oak and made entirely with jointed pieces with no screws or nails, as well as large cupboards, which are veritable sculptures.

In the office there is a series of chairs and tables in carved wood and in organic forms, the originals of which are kept by the current owners and which have been reproduced and commercialised with notable success. The visiting room was on the first floor, the furniture of which is currently in the Gaudí House-Museum in Park Güell, and is made of gilded wood and rich upholstery consisting of sofa, armchairs, chairs, stools and a mirror.

In 1900 the City Council created the prize for the best building build in the city during the year and the winner that year was in fact Casa Calvet.

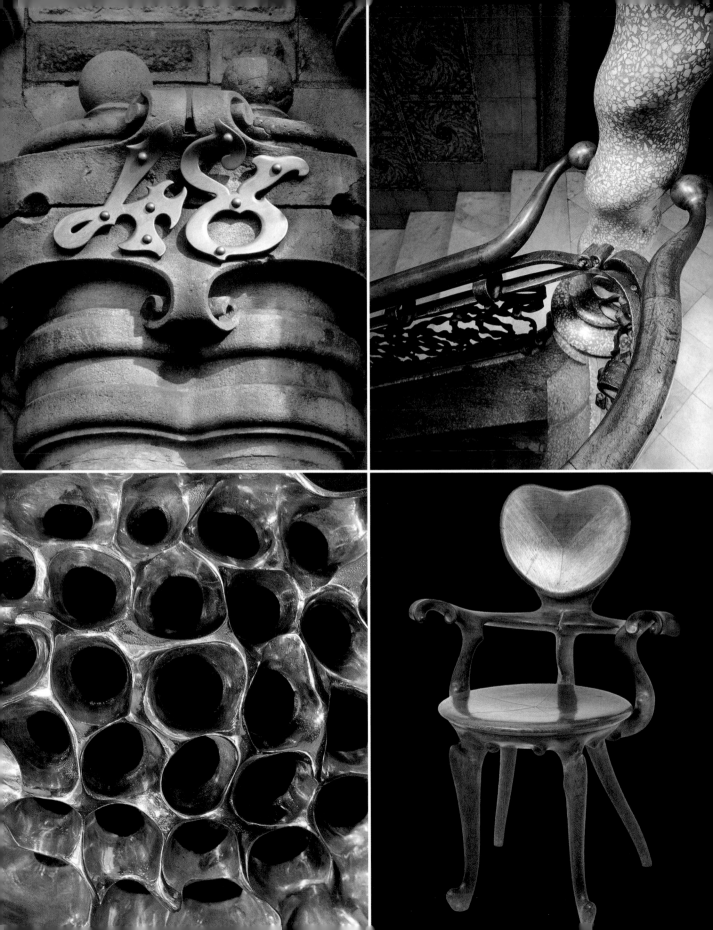

2  3
4  5

2  **Detail of the façade**
3  **Detail of the handrail**
4  **Peephole of naturalist inspiration**
5  **Chair designed by Gaudí**

6  **Anagram of Calvet with a cypress tree**

6

## ⑩ Bellesguard Tower Barcelona

In the high part of the Sant Gervasi district of Barcelona the widow of Jaume Figueras had a piece of land on which stood some ruins of what was called the Royal Palace of Bellesguard, a country house ordered to be built by King Martí I of the Crown of Aragon in 1410 and which he gave the name *Bellesguard* (beautiful view in English) at the request of his secretary, the poet Bernat Metge.

This is the palace where King Martí I married his second wife Margarida de Prades, a wedding officiated by the antipope Benedict XIII. For this historical reason Gaudí conceived a building inspired by late Catalan Gothic.

The building made up of a ground floor, first floor, second floor and attic is built with brick and the exterior rendered with slate dug from the site so that it fully identifies with its natural environment. The building has a square ground plan and the diagonals mark the cardinal points. On the left corner of the main façade there is a tower that rises 35 metres over the ground and culminates with a pyramid trunk shape, on the upper part of which can be seen the Catalan flag with the bars in helicoidal form, a crown and a four-armed cross.

The crown is blue, the flag red and gold and the cross white. This chromatism is achieved by simply rendering fragments of glass painted on the side attached to the tower with limestone mortar.

Inside, the building is plastered with a permanent white over undulating forms in the arches and walls. Outstanding here are the two superimposed attics, the lower one with a series of 10 cm brick arch ribs which sprout from a central structure and lead to the walls of the façade. The second attic is formed by a bricked cloister vault.

A parapet walk with different stairways surrounds the second attic which has crenellations all around the walls' perimeter.

To join Bellesguard with the ruins of a tower, between 1903 and 1905, Gaudí rerouted an old path that went past the property and supported it over a vault held up by leaning pillars, creating a viaduct similar to those in Park Güell.

Gaudí worked on Bellesguard between 1900 and 1909 although the building, the garden benches and façade were completed later by Gaudí's assistant architect Domènec Sugrañes Gras.

2 **Venus, the star of twilight in reference to Martí I, the last king of the Catalan dynasty**

3 **Ribs on the ceiling of the second floor**

4 **Parapet walkway of the flat roof**

5 **Tri-lobed arches of parabolic form in the first attic**

2

3

4

5

# ⑪ **Park Güell** Barcelona

In 1899 Eusebi Güell bought some land in the town of Gràcia, in the area of the Salut district, a piece of land known as the Can Muntaner de Dalt as well as the Bald Mountain, the name given to it by the Hieronymite monks from the monastery in Val d'Hebró in memory of Golgotha, the place where Christ was crucified.

Güell chose this land, until then the property of the Marquis of Marianao, for its geographical similarity to the Greek city of Delphi, where the poetry festivals were held in honour of Apollo. At the foot of Mount Parnassus was the Doric temple of Apollo in whose omphalus the sun god buried the evil dragon Python, who became the protector of the underground waters that emerged in the thermal springs of Cassotis, Delphi and Castalia, giving inspiration to the sibyls or prophetesses. Güell wanted to link this symbolism of Hellenic culture with the Christian and nationalist feeling of Catalonia.

In Park Güell stands the Hypostyle hall of Doric order, the only case whereby Gaudí used classical orders, the dragon Python who spits out the water from the overflow of the tank beneath the temple, the tripod from where the sibyls launched their oracles and the source of high iron content water that was sold bottled by the name of Agua Sarva. Christianity is present in the Calvary, the chapel of the Güell house, the Rosary whose beads are balls of stone on the sides of the paths and the crosses in the entrance pavilions. In the middle of the stairway a ceramic mosaic with the four masts of Aragon show the relationship of Christian Catalonia with classical Greek culture, inspired by the *Renaixença*.

Special mention should be made of the winding bench that encloses the square and in which Josep Maria Jujol produced a work of unbounded imagination, where the collage of *trencadís* mosaic of ceramic and glass reach their maximum expression.

Another aspect is the exquisite solutions for the viaducts, the broken ceramic tiling or the wise solutions for channelling water that Gaudí came up with. The park has been council property since 1923, became a national monument 1969 and has been a World Heritage Site since 1984. This garden city project begun in 1900 in the high part of Barcelona failed in its attempt to see 60 isolated houses. Due to the distance from the city centre and the restrictive conditions imposed by Güell in the sale of the sites, only three buildings were actually inhabited.

1 **Stairway and hypostyle hall**                    Carrer Olot, s/n

2 **Battlemented balcony of the porter's pavilion**
3 **Ground floor of the services pavilion**
4 **Roof of the porter's pavilion**
5 **Interior of the porter's pavilion, the Park Güell Information Centre**

2

3

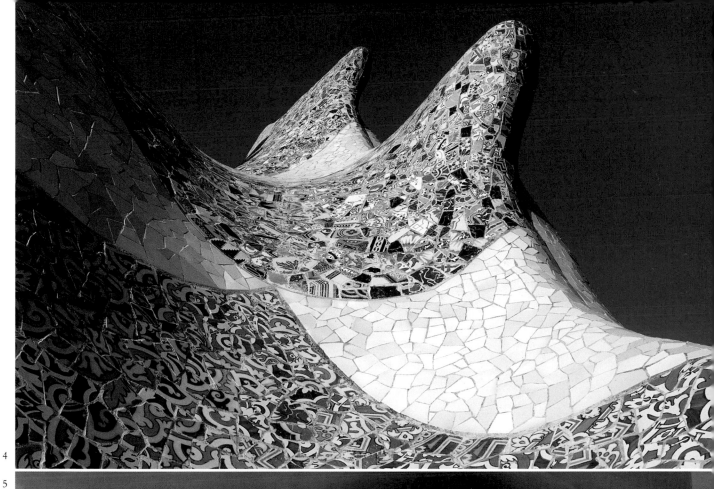

4

5

6

6 Aerial view of the
   square and entrance

7 Dragon of the stairway

8 The round shields
   represent suns and
   moons

7

8

9

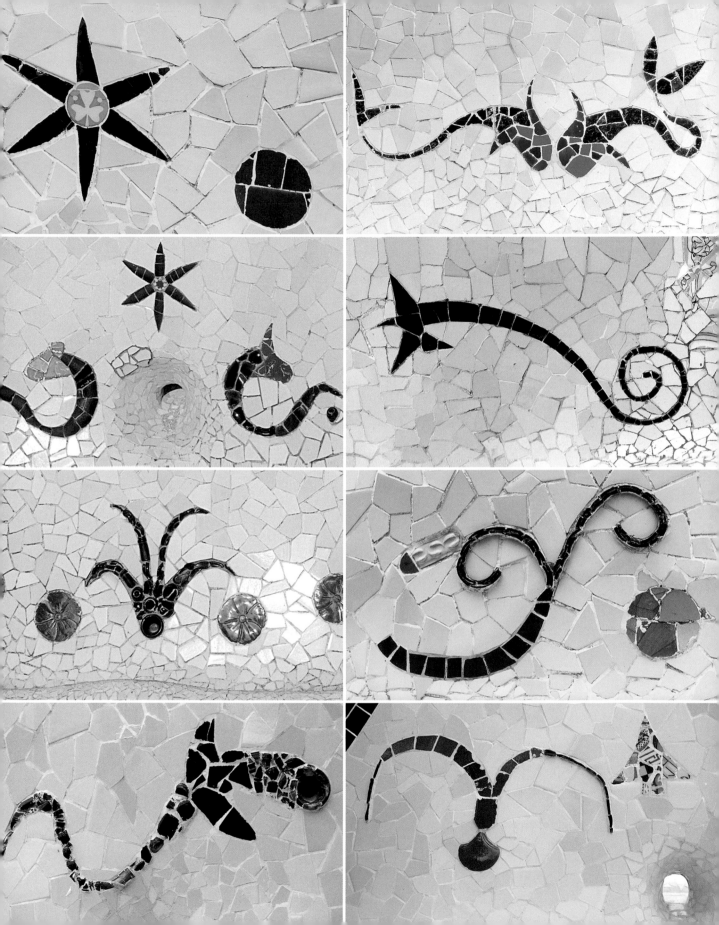

11 **Leaning columns in the Washerwoman's arcade**

12 **Helicoidal columns**

13 **Caryatid known as the Washerwoman**

14 **Pots with pitas**

15 **The Calvary at the top of the park**

11

12   13

14

15

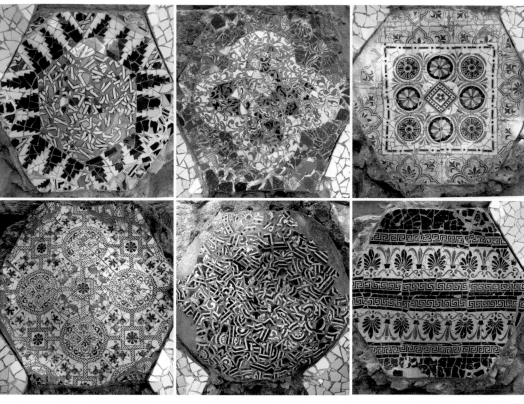

16 **Soffits of original** *trencadís* **in the Gaudí House-Museum**

17 **Room of the Gaudí House-Museum with the famous benches and chairs from Casa Batlló**

18 **Gaudí House-Museum**

16

17

18

# ⑫ **Cathedral** Palma de Mallorca

The precise time period for the restoration of the Cathedral of Mallorca was between 1904 and 1914. The then Bishop of Mallorca, Pere Campins Barceló (1859-1915), came up with the idea of restoring his cathedral and on passing through Barcelona on the 18 August 1901, visited the works of the Temple of the Sagrada Família and had a long exchange of ideas with Antoni Gaudí.

Gaudí prepared his project, which along general lines consisted of taking down the Baroque altarpiece from the high altar, along with the rest of the Gothic parts joined to its rear section, leaving in view the Episcopal Chair, work of Bishop Berenguer de Balle which was inaugurated on 1 October 1346, move the choir from the centre of the nave and place it in the presbytery, leave clear the chapel of the Trinity, place new choir stalls and pulpits, decorate the cathedral appropriately with electric lighting, reopen the Gothic windows of the Royal Chapel and give them stained-glass windows, place a large baldachin over the high altar and complete the decoration with paintings, curtains, etc. He also planned the installation of the tombs of the kings of Mallorca, Jaume II and Jaume III, in the chapel of the Trinity.

On the 31 October 1903 Gaudí was in Palma in the company of the architect Joan Rubió Bellver (1870-1952), his main collaborator on this work, with several samples of glass for the stained-glass windows and the full restoration project.

The chronological description of the works begins on the 19 June 1904, the day when Rubió arrived in Palma to start the work, and ends on the day of the Immaculate Conception, the 8 December 1914, in which the first stage of the works was officially opened.

The choir has been moved, the Baroque altar moved and installed in a church in the Santa Catalina district, the Gothic altarpiece placed above the Mirador doorway and the Episcopal chair given new importance by surrounding it with phrases from the ritual of bishops, made from gilded iron, as well as placing the elegant baldachin, the choir stalls and pulpits, still not completely finished.

As well as Joan Rubió, the painter Jaume Llongueras came as a collaborator of Gaudí on this first stage, which is the best documented and most well-known. From 1905 the enthusiasm of the Chapter for the restoration gradually waned until in spring 1914 Gaudí abandoned the work, which had been left unfinished. Suffice to say that the baldachin is provisional and he had been expecting to make in iron what now is only wood and cardboard.

Between 1905 and 1914 Gaudí tried to continue with the works and to do this he managed to obtain the cooperation of such important artists as the sculptor from Igualada Vicenç Vilarrubias Valls, the Uruguayan painter Joaquín Torres García (1875-1949), the painter Ivo Pascual Rodés (1883-1949), the already mentioned Jaume Llongueras Badía and finally the highly individualistic Josep Maria Jujol Gibert (1879-1949), distinguished architect, painter and chromatist. Between 1907 and 1908 Torres, Pascual and Llongueras composed the stained-glass windows for Palma in the workshop of the Sagrada Família in Barcelona. Jujol painted the choir stalls based on stains and gilts with almost illegible inscriptions, of a really impressive strength. The effect is marvellous, but did not convince the members of the Chapter who were shocked by this surge of colour and form emphasised by the gold.

The good canons of Mallorca were shocked and feared that if they gave Gaudí and Jujol free reign they would end up by polychroming the entire cathedral.

Gaudí did not only concern himself with the architecture and decoration, but also the furnishing and liturgical objects. He designed the high altar using some Gothic angels. He made the handrail of the presbytery and the foldaway staircase to it. He designed the ciborium, the tintinabulum and other objects, many of which are kept in the Diocesan Museum.

1 **Baldachin**

2 **Forms typical of Jujol's style**

3 **Foldaway stairs for exhibiting the Holy Sacrament**

4 and 7 **Inscriptions in forged iron and gilt**

5 **Gestural painting on the choir stalls**

6 **Episcopal shield**

2
3

4 5
6 7

# ⑬ Casa Batlló Barcelona

A simple reform of the façade, new distribution of the partition walls and an enlargement of the well of a building originally built in 1875, gave Gaudí the chance to undertake one of his most poetic and inspired artistic compositions. A stone thrown into a pond full of flowering water lilies would produce the same effect as that of the main façade of Casa Batlló, of an undulating surface covered with polychrome circles of glazed ceramics and different coloured fragments of broken glass, the exact position of which Gaudí personally oversaw from the street.

The double attic that culminates the façade has a twofold character: animalistic and legendary, having supplied people's imaginations with the most outrageous interpretations of a supposed dragon fighting Saint George, although the Saint cannot be seen anywhere around, while in a small cylindrical tower which hides a spiral staircase, the anagrams are clearly seen of Jesus, Mary and Joseph, in ivory-coloured glazed ceramic, with the special Gaudian calligraphy, arranged helicoidally below a four-armed cross in Mallorca ceramics. The symbol is therefore of the Holy Family rather than Saint George.

The façade of the first floor, which was the home of the Batlló family, is of sandstone carved with lively forms, supported by thin columns with plant motifs and it also has the elegant carpentry of the large windows and the leaded stained-glass windows of lively colours, arranged in a warped form. The joy that this project gives off can also be clearly seen in the bright and polychrome rear façade adorned with multiple broken ceramic flowers which give it a naive and happy air, just like the chimneys on the flat roof and in the chromatic harmony of the well, covered with blue glazed tiles that darken in tone the higher up they are. If one had to define Casa Batlló in any way, it would be by saying that it is an architectural smile, an explosion of compositional pleasure by someone who is in full control of their very own personal style, which enables them to disconnect from pre-existent philosophies.

The work undertaken, between 1904 and 1906,

1 **Private staircase with the form of a vertebrate's spine**

Passeig de Gràcia, 43

consisted of enlarging the inner courtyard, changing the low part of the main façade completely, changing the appearance of the front and back façades, crowning the front façade with the double attic of catenary arches and brickwork panels covered in the area of the flat roof with broken polychrome tiling and on the street part with roof tiles of fish scales in changing colours, crowned by a kind of backbone of almost spherical pieces and others in the form of half rods of different colours that, from one end to the ridge to the other have yellow, green and blue tones, with large-scale pieces. For the railings of the cast iron balconies, he made a full-size plaster model in the workshops of the Sagrada Família, which were then sent to the foundry. This ledge, repeated seven times, plus another larger one on the small terrace on the fourth floor, is attached to the wall by means of just two anchorages, the entire railing projecting without support on the flagstone of the sculpted sandstone balcony. On the terraces there are Carrara white marble balusters, also helicoidal in shape. The

columns of Montjuïc stone of the ground floor, those of the first floor and those of the two first-floor galleries, were the object of plaster model studies in order to outline the slender osseous forms decorated with plant motifs. The result was five hollow spaces that seem like mouths, which gave the building the popular name of the "House of yawns".

The courtyard is covered with a two-sided skylight supported with laminated iron parabolic arches. This latter floor was initially used for services and laundries but, in 1983, the lower attic was restored and turned into a small museum. The rest of the floor has been accessible since 1998 on extending the lift situated in the courtyard and can be visited by tourists, as an anteroom to the route via the flat roof where one can see the polychromed chimneys.

In the 1991 restoration, the dining room recovered its original appearance, but without the table, chairs and benches that were acquired by the Friends of Gaudí and are today on show in the Gaudí House-Museum in Park Güell.

2

3

2 **Lobby**

3 **Upper part of the façade**

4

5

6

7

8

9  10

Gaudí Casa Batlló  **87**
Casa Batlló

8  **Attic**
9  **Attic corridor**
10  **Stairway to the flat roof**
11  **The blue on the higher part of the skylight is a deeper colour**

11

12 **Chimneys**
13 **Roof**
14 **Rear courtyard**

12

13                                              14

# ⑭ La Pedrera Barcelona

When, at the end of 1905 Josep Bayó Font was finishing the decoration of the Batlló family residence for Gaudí, he was visited by Pere Milà Camps. Bayó showed him the flat and on bidding farewell, Milà gave him a pat on the back, saying, "Now we must start on my house on the corners of Passeig de Gràcia and Carrer Provença and I want it in stone but with the joints gilded, something that has never been done before". It is true that Gaudí built Casa Milà, called the La Pedrera, or the quarry, with stone, but the gilded joints were no more than a frivolity of the stylish client.

On the 2 February 1906 Gaudí signed the project contract for the house of his new client and began his second big civil work in the stately Barcelona avenue. According to José Bayó, an eyewitness, Gaudí put his fingers in the hexagonal wax model of the paving stones, which were made on the site of Casa Batlló itself. The piece of hydraulic mosaic in relief and of a pale green colour draws, when seven units are pieced together, a triple drawing representing an algae (Sargassum species), a snail (cephalopod of the Ammonites family) and a sea star (Equinodermus,

of the Ophiroideus family). Pere Milà Camps married Pilar Segimon Artells, a lady born in Reus and widow of a rich *indiano*, a Spaniard who returned to Spain having made his fortune in Latin America. The lady was not keen on Gaudí's ideas, but to keep her husband happy, she lived in the first floor flat of La Pedrera without complaining but, on Gaudí's death, she changed the decoration for another Louis XVI style, more to her taste.

Casa Milà occupies part of Passeig de Gràcia, the corner and a large part of Carrer Provença. It is a house for rented flats with a lower ground floor that was for storage and garages, a mezzanine for offices, the first floor given over entirely for the home of the Milà family, with an independent stairway via the courtyard in Carrer Provença, four floors with two flats per landing, with entry via a lift next to the corner street and a service stairway at the end of this courtyard. On the top is the attic of brickwork catenary arches that was for the laundries and storage, below the flat roof, with the eight stairways, ventilators and chimneys that have made the house famous.

1 **Aerial view of the flat roof**
Passeig de Gràcia, 92

The façades in Passeig de Gràcia and Provença are made of stone from Vilafranca, cut in huge blocks and joined to the iron main beam and joists that form the structure of the building supported on brick, stone or cast iron pillars.

In terms of the flats, Gaudí designed them as a series of spaces joined to each other by partitions with large windows that enabled one to see the whole flat from one end to the other. Light freely penetrates through the large windows and balcony doors that lead to the terraces, where the twisted iron railings designed by Jujol are placed. The ceilings of the corridors and rooms are in plaster and relief, all different and sculpted with forms and inscriptions that produce a pleasant sensation of harmony and gentle movement.

The Milà family refused to have the building crowned by a sculptural group over four metres high of the Virgin and Child. Today, beneath the monogram of Maria, we find a rose in stone, a Marian allegory.

Today the building is owned by the Caixa Catalunya banking entity, which, after restoring it, has fitted out a space for temporary and one permanent exhibition: the Espai Gaudí.

2

3

4

5

6

7

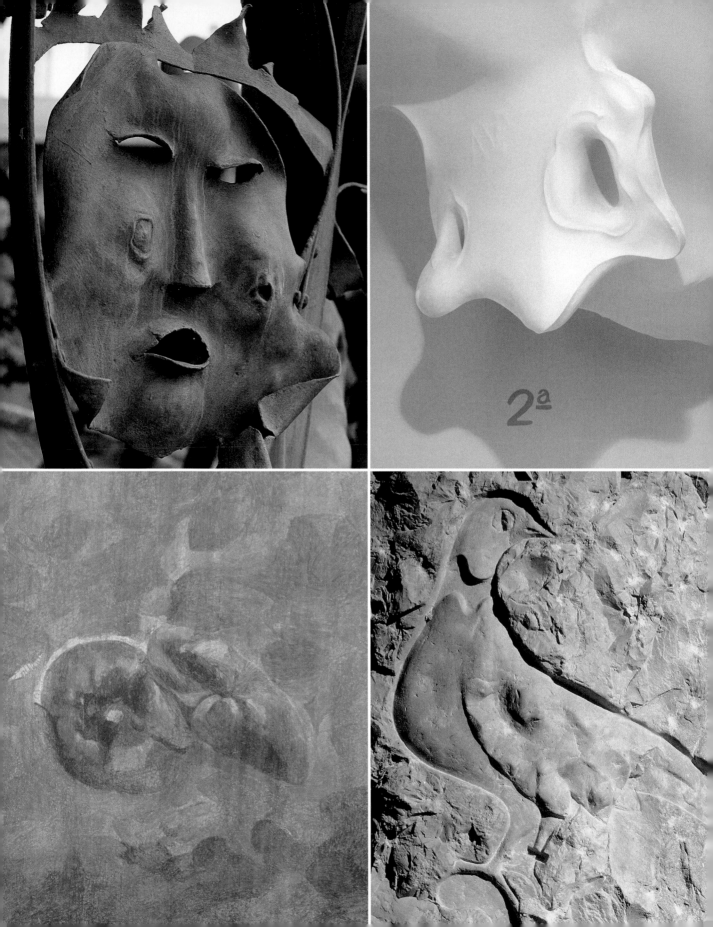

| 8 9 |
|-----|
| 10 11 |

8 **Mask on a balcony**

9 **Emerging form in the lintel of a door with the inscription "Ave"**

10 **Mural painting**

11 **Column of the main floor**

12, 13 and 14 **Attic, currently the Espai Gaudí**

12

13

14

19

5  16

7  18

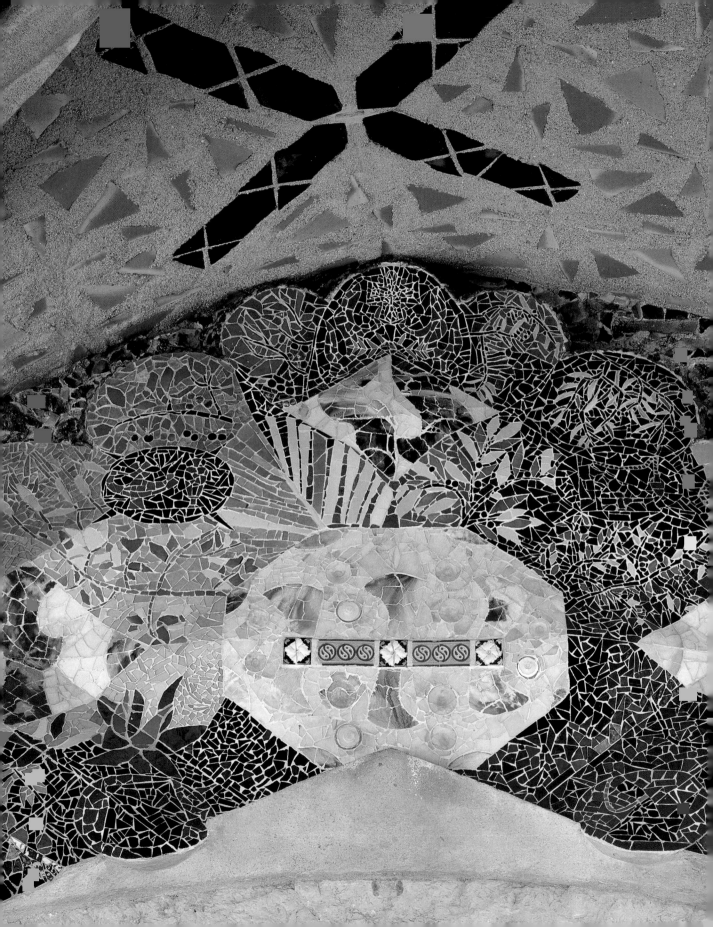

# ⑮ Church of the Colònia Güell

## Santa Coloma de Cervelló

This church was for the workers of the Colònia Güell industrial village (Santa Coloma de Cervelló, Barcelona), from which it gets its name.

The church of Santa Coloma became one of the most-loved of Gaudí's projects, and was a type of laboratory for technical tests, of which he later made use of in the Sagrada Família.

Gaudí's idea is extremely complex, and the church was designed and detailed with the utmost care. Once again the architect thought about the need to unite the monument with its natural setting, and this is the only compositional element used in this work. According to Ràfols the commission for the job dates back to 1898, but it was not until 1908 that the first stone was solemnly laid. The work continued at a very slow pace until 1917, when they were stopped due to the difficulties arising from the Great War. In 1918 Eusebi Güell died in his home in Park Güell, which also meant the end of the work on the church of the industrial village since his heirs, particularly Santiago Güell, were not at all keen on finishing the building. By then the crypt was covered and the stone doorways of the upper church in place. The conception of this church followed lines until then unknown by the architectural profession.

Gaudí did not limit himself to drawing and sketching, but tested out a completely new procedure. Firstly he outlined the ideal form of the church that had to have a concentrated ground plan and acute towers; over this first draft Gaudí composed a structure by means of a very simple, but quite brilliant, procedure. He calculated the loads that would have to rest on the arches and pillars and made some small canvas bags filled with pellets, with a weight ten thousand times lighter than the calculated load. He hung these bags from strings that described the forms of the arches at a scale of 1:10. With this, and using a geometric property of this type of curve, he discovered a form called catenary. He took a photograph, which on reversing produced the suitable and functional form of the arches. In other words, he built the arch precisely from the form of the curve of the pressures.

The crypt of the Colònia Güell brings together Gaudí's artistic plenitude. A portico with paraboloid vaults precedes the church and below another is in the form of a grotto, a constant element in the architecture of Gaudí. The windows, which seem like

the open mouths of giant fish, are hyperboloids, and inside the pillars alternate between circular section brick and inclined natural basalt stone from Castell-follit de la Roca (Garrotxa), hardly smoothed down, giving an impressive expressionist effect. Gaudí explained that in the book of Exodus, God, from the burning bush, said to Moses, "If you make me an altar of stone do no carve it with a chisel because metal makes stone impure". For this reason the pieces of basalt were worked with wooden mallets.

The ceiling is made up of a series of brick ribs over which is supported the base of the upper flooring.

The brick pillars are plastered to a certain height and over them are drawn catenary forms in relief. The ribs and the intrados of the floor support had to be plastered with Portland cement, but only a small part was done, the rest being done in open brickwork.

Another remarkable aspect of the crypt is the abundant Christian iconography it contains: fish, the letters alpha and omega, which represent the beginning and the end, crosses, monograms of Christ, Saint Andrew's crosses, etc.

The crypt of the Colònia Güell seems more like a sculpture than an architectural work and even more than a sculpture, seems to be a living thing, with its tensed muscles, working to withstand its own weight and energy.

The crypt of the Colònia Güell is a monument that it is an absolute must to see in order to understand not only the figure of Gaudí but also the very history of architecture.

2 **Defective bricks and slag combined with mosaics in *trencadís***

3 **General view**

4 **Vaults of the portico**

2

3

4

5  Interior of the crypt

# ⑯ Temple of the Sagrada Família
## Barcelona

Josep Maria Bocabella Verdaguer (1815-1892) was a bookshop owner who, moved by his great mercy, was inspired and felt the vehement desire to organise what he gave the name to of the Association of Devotees of Saint Joseph.

In 1881 the Association bought a whole block of Barcelona's Eixample district within the municipality of Sant Martí de Provençals.

The early project for the Expiatory Temple of the Sagrada Família was produced by the architect Francesc de Paula del Villar y Lozano in 1882, a project that was interrupted in 1883 after the disagreements between Villar and the architect advising Bocabella, Joan Martorell Montells.

The direction of the works was offered to Martorell who for reasons of politeness did not accept, but he proposed his former assistant Antoni Gaudí. From then on the temple took on a different form and spirit, the Villar project being consigned to oblivion.

On taking over the works Gaudí regretted the arrangement of the crypt since he would have preferred to orientate the building diagonally across the block. On not being able to put his idea into practice he limited himself to surrounding the crypt with a large ditch, making it no longer a basement, and finishing it without introducing variants other than changing the motifs of the capitals which lost their Corinthian appearance to become naturalist interpretations of the flora.

In May 1885 Gaudí signed the project for the ground plan of the Sagrada Família which he used to ask for the works permit in the Sant Martí Council. There is no evidence to show that the council approved it.

In 1892 work began on the Nativity Façade. Two years later the neo-Gothic apse was completed in which wheatears of the pinnacles and the gargoyles of amphibians and reptiles underlined the naturalist tendency of the decoration which the Nativity Façade would have. The first bell tower of this façade was completed in 1925. Gaudí expressed his joy on see-

1  **Knots in the columns of the central nave**

Nativity Façade. Carrer Marina, 253

ing, "how that spear joined heaven with the earth". The architect could not continue his work since he died the following year. Nevertheless, in 1923, he came up with the definitive solution for the naves and roofing in plaster models at scale 1:10 and 1:25. The models that Gaudí left, partly destroyed during the Civil War, have enabled the works to be continued and can be seen in the Sagrada Família Museum.

The Expiatory Temple of the Sagrada Família, the construction of which continues in line with the spirit of Gaudí, is a church with five naves, with three façades, Nativity, Passion and Glory at the ends of the crossing and foot of the church. It is surrounded by a cloister and will have a large stairway facing the Glory Façade where there will be a cresset and a fountain in front of the baptism and communion chapels. Two large sacristies flank the apse, in the middle of which will figure the chapel of the Assumption. Eighteen towers are built in honour of Jesus Christ, the Virgin, the Apostles and the Evangelists. Gaudí conceived this temple not only as an expression of his naturalist architecture but also as a biblical text in architectural form.

2  **Linking bridge between the towers**

3  **Nativity Façade**

2    3

4  **Trumpeting angel**

5  **Constellation
of Gemini in the
sculptural group of
the signs of the zodiac**

6  **Sculptural group of
the Nativity**

7  **Chameleon in the
cloister**

8  **Charity Doorway**

8

11

12

13

14

ES QUAN AQUELL DISSABTE ERA UN
A DA SOLEMNÍSSIMA PER AIXO EL
JEUS VAN DEMANAR A PILAT QU
ER QUESSIN LES CAMES DES CRUCIFICA
RAGUESSIN ELS SEUS COSSOS HI HAN ARRI
ONCS ELS SOLDATS VAN TRENCAR LE
MES DEL PRIMER I EL DE LA TREQU
VIA ESTAT CRUCIFICAT AMB JESUS
UAN ARRIBAREN A JESUS ES VA
DO MAR QUE JA ERA MORT I NO LI TRE
AREN LES CAMES PERO UN DELS SOLDA
RA SPASSA EL COSTAT AMB LA LLANÇ
I SANG I AIGUA TOT AIXO VA SUCCEI
RQUE S'HAVIA DE COMPLIR ALO QUE D
SCRIPTURA NO LI HAN DE TRENC
P.OS DESPRES JOSEP D'ARIMATE
JE ERA DEIXEBLE D JESUS PERO D'AMAG
RPORA DEMANAR A PILAT AUTORITZAC
RA TREURE EL SEU COS DE LA CR
PI LAT HI VA ACCEDIR JOSEP DON
VA TREURE L DE LA CREU EL C

18

17

19 Arboreal columns

20 Knots in the columns of the central nave

21 Ceiling of the schools

22 Undulating roof of the schools that impressed Le Corbusier and which in their apparent simplicity show the expressive and structural strength of using ruled surfaces, in this case conoid

19

20

21

22

1 **First Mystery of Glory in Montserrat**

2 **Bridge in the Artigas gardens**

3 **Doorway of the Miralles estate**

4 **Tile designed by Gaudí**

1

2

# Other works

In 1902 Gaudí visited the mountainous area of La Pobla de Lillet (Berguedà). In this wild spot he planned a garden that has two stone bridges over the River Llobregat, diverse sculptures and arbours. Of a decidedly romantic air, it was made by labourers who worked on the Park Güell site. It was not identified as a work by Gaudí until 1973 and, since then has been replanted, restored and made accessible via an old mining railway.

The Canon of Vic, Jaume Collell Bancels proposed the construction of the fifteen stations of the Rosary of Montserrat along the Santa Cova pathway where the image of the Virgin was found. Different devout congregations and individuals financed the construction of the monuments corresponding to the Mysteries of the Rosary. In 1903 the "Spiritual League of the Mother of God of Montserrat" entrusted Gaudí with the project for the First Mystery of the Glory, the Resurrection of Christ and he composed an ar-

chitectural piece without any elements other than a grotto excavated from the mountainside where the empty sepulchre of Christ was situated, with the three Marys and above, the figure of the resuscitated Christ, a piece in bronze by Josep Llimona Bruguera.

Hermenegild Miralles Anglès was a publisher, manufacturer of "papier maché" floor tiles and a good friend of Gaudí to whom he commissioned, in 1902, the enclosing wall and entrance doorway to his estate in the Güell private road en Sarrià. It is a wall of curved lines and surfaces according to the Gaudian concept of plane architecture built with masonry ashlar crowned with plastered curved surfaces and metal fabric grilles. It has two doors, for carriages and pedestrians, with a protective roof of metallic structures and pebble fibre-cement tiles similar to tortoiseshell. Above there is a three-dimensional metallic cross.

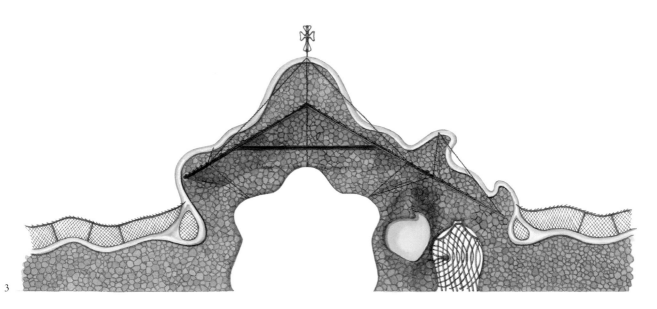

3

### Chronology

**1852**

Antoni Gaudí was born in Reus.

**1867**

With Eduard Toda and Josep Ribera, he conceives a restoration plan for the monastery of Poblet.

**1869**

He moves to Barcelona with his brother Francesc.

**1872**

He enrols at the Higher School of Architecture of Barcelona.

**1876**

The deaths of his brother, Francesc, and his mother have a profound effect on the young Gaudí's state of mind and he seeks refuge in his architectural studies. From this period are preserved projects such as the cemetery gate or the jetty.

To pay for his studies, he works with the architects Francesc de P. Del Villar and Eduard Fontseré who he helped in Ciutadella Park where he produced, among other pieces, the two naturalist panels at the Aquarium entrance, which is behind the monumental waterfall.

**1877**

He finishes the graduate project for a university auditorium.

**1878**

He creates a display cabinet for the Comella glove shop, exhibited at the Universal Exhibition of Paris.

He completes his studies at the School of Architecture. The principal, Elies Rogent, states, "I don't know whether we have given the qualification to a madman or a genius".

He designs the Girossi news stand and lampposts for Barcelona City Council. After seeing the Comella display cabinet, Eusebi Güell takes an interest in Gaudí's work and commissions him with the liturgical furniture for the chapel of Antonio López in Comillas.

He undertakes several projects for the Mataró Co-operative Society of which the watercolour that was shown at the Universal Exhibition of Paris still survives.

**1879**

Gaudí's sister dies and he takes over the guardianship of his niece Rosa Egea. He decorates the Gibert pharmacy and joins the Catalan Association for Scientific Excursions.

**1881**

He publishes an article in the magazine *La Renaixença*. He builds a news stand to commemorate the visit of King Alfons XII to Comillas.

**1882**

He draws up the project of Joan Martorell who took part in a bid for the facade of the cathedral of Barcelona and designs a hunting lodge for the property of Eusebi Güell in Garraf. Neither project is ever realised.

### 1883

Proposed by Joan Martorell, Gaudí replaces F. del Villar as head of the works of the Sagrada Família.

He begins work on the Casa Vicens and El Capricho in Comillas. As his assistant, he employs a young man aged 17, Francesc Berenguer.

He uses the catenary arch for the first time in the bleaching room of the Mataró Co-operative.

### 1884

He signs the first official document as architect of the Sagrada Família. He begins the pavilions of the Güell estate in Les Corts.

### 1885

First full project for the Sagrada Família.

He designs the Dragon Gateway of the Güell Pavilions.

### 1886

After producing several design variations of the Palau Güell facade, Gaudí, helped by Berenguer, comes up with a solution that he presents to Barcelona City Council.

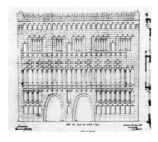

He begins construction work of the Palau Güell.

### 1887

With Domènech i Montaner he travels to Manises (Valencia) in order to learn the traditional techniques of glazed pottery. He finishes the pavilions of the Güell estate.

### 1888

He makes the pavilion for the Compañía Transatlántica in the Universal exhibition of Barcelona. He makes a project for the decoration – unrealised – of the Saló de Cent (Council Chamber). He completes the Casa Vicens and Enric d'Ossó commissions him with the work for the Theresan College.

### 1890

The trips to León and Astorga begin. Joan Baptista Grau, the bishop of Astorga, has a profound influence on Gaudí's religious thinking. He finishes the Theresan College.

**1891**

Gaudí signs the project for the Casa Botines in León.

**1892**

He builds the Casa Botines in ten months.

He starts the project for the Nativity Façade. The apse of the Sagrada Família reaches a height of 20 metres.

**1893**

He abandons the work on the Episcopal Palace of Astorga without finishing the roofing.

He undertakes the project for the Franciscan Catholic Missions of Tangier in Africa which, while never being realised, shows a similarity to the temple of the Sagrada Família.

He finishes the apse of the temple.

**1894**

The foundations of the Nativity Façade are completed and its construction begins.

A Lent fast puts the architect's life at risk. Bishop Torres i Bages persuades him to abandon the penitence.

**1895**

He plans the Güell Bodegas in Garraf.

**1898**

He presents the project for the Casa Calvet.

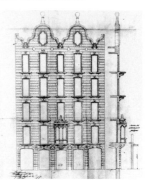

He begins the studies for the construction of the church of the Güell Industrial Village and the development of the polyfunicular model.

**1899**

He joins two Catalan institutions with a catholic ideology: The Artistic Circle of Sant Lluc and the Spiritual league of the Virgin of Montserrat, which commissions Gaudí to build the First Mystery of Glory.

## 1900

He starts work on Bellesguard and Park Güell. He completes the Casa Calvet, which receives the prize from the City Council for the best building in Barcelona.

Some sculptures are placed on the Nativity Façade. Donations for the temple run short.

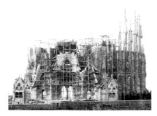

## 1902

He builds the doorway for the estate of H. Miralles and takes part in the decoration of the Café Torino (no longer in existence).

## 1904

He embarks on the reform of the cathedral of Mallorca and of the Casa Batlló for which he draws up a draft project that differs greatly from the final result.

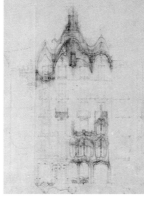

At the behest of Lluís Graner, he decorates the Sala Mercè, one of the first cinemas in Barcelona.

Project that was never realised, also by Lluís Graner, for a chalet in the Bonanova district.

## 1905

He produces the Catllaràs chalet and the gardens of Can Artigues in La Pobla de Lillet.

## 1906

An original sketch by Gaudí of the Temple of the complete Sagrada Família is published.

He moves, with his father and niece, to the house in Park Güell built by Berenguer. His father dies on the 29th of October.

Construction work begins on the Casa Milà, "La Pedrera".

## 1907

He finishes the Casa Batlló.

**1908**

After ten years of studies, work starts on the church of Güell Industrial Village. According to Joan

Matamala, Gaudí received the commission from the North Americans to build a hotel in New York. Matamala reproduced the project in a drawing.

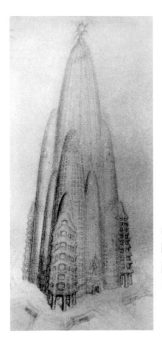

**1909**

He build and self-finances the schools for the Temple of the Sagrada Família.

He finishes his work on Bellesgard and leaves his collaborator Sugrañcs to finish off somc details.

**1910**

A polychrome model of the Nativity Façade is exhibited in Paris.

Gaudí rests in Vic to recover from anaemia and designs, together with Jujol and Canaleta, some lampposts for the town's main square and which would disappear in 1924.

**1911**

Gaudí falls ill with brucellosis and is taken to Puigcerdà to recover. While there, he plans the Passion Façade.

**1912**

His niece, Rosa Egea, dies. He finishes the Casa Milà.

**1913**

The undulating bench in Park Güell is completed on which the collaboration of Jujol is evident.

**1914**

He finishes the work on Park Güell. Work is halted on the church of the Güell industrial Village. His friend and collaborator F. Berenguer dies. Gaudí devotes his time to the Sagrada Família.

## 1915

He undertakes a rehearsal with tubular bells in the towers of the Sagrada Família.

## 1916

The lack of donations to build the Sagrada Família forces Gaudí to make street collections. This circumstance is both satirised and politicised by the republican press of the time which publishes a cartoon strip in which Güell heads a procession of outstanding figures who beg for charity with the temple in the background.

## 1918

Eusebi Güell Bacigalupi dies.

## 1923

Definitive solution for the naves and roofing in 1:10 and 1:25 scale plaster models.

The central bell towers of the Nativity Façade reach a height of eighty metres.

## 1924

On the eleventh of September Gaudí is arrested when he goes to a mass held in honour of the Catalans who fell in defence of Barcelona in 1714.

## 1925

The tower of St. Barnabus is completed on the 30th of November with the pinnacle. Gaudí exclaims his joy, "on seeing how that lance joins the heavens with the earth".

Gaudí moves to the Sagrada Família workshops.

## 1926

Gaudí dies after being run over by a tram. The streets of Barcelona are filled with people who accompany the funeral procession. The architect was buried in the crypt of the Sagrada Família.

© Triangle Postals

© **Texts**
Joan Bassegoda i Nonell

© **Photography**
Pere Vivas
Ricard Pla
Rafael Vargas (56, 58b)
Biel Puig (97b, 103b)
Jordi Puig, Pere Vivas (76, 78, 79)
Casa Batlló (80, 81, 82, 83, 84, 85, 86, 87, 88, 89)
Pere Vivas / Junta Constructora del Temple de la Sagrada Família (106, 108, 109, 110, 111, 112, 113, 114, 115, 116, 117, 118, 119)

© **Illustrations**
Dissenys Papeti SL

© **Archive photographs**
Arxiu de la Reial Càtedra Gaudí
Arxiu Històric de la Ciutat de Barcelona
Temple expiatori de la Sagrada Família
Ricard Opisso, VEGAP, Barcelona 2007
Museu Comarcal Salvador Vilaseca. Reus

© **Translation**
Steve Cedar

**Design**
Joan Colomer

**Layout**
Mercè Camerino, Aina Pla

**Printed by**
Tallers gràfics Soler
9/2008

**Registration number**
B-24635-2007

**ISBN**
978-84-8478-279-7


**TRIANGLE POSTALS, SL**
Sant Lluís
Menorca
Tel. +34 971 15 04 51
Fax +34 971 15 18 36
www.triangle.cat

Acknowledgements:

Luís Guilera Soler, Torre de Bellesguard
Família Herrero, Casa Vicens
Carme Hosta
Anna Ribas
Teresa Martínez de Dalmases
Laia Vinaixa
Masako Yamauchi, El Capricho

Capítol de la Catedral de Mallorca
Casa-Museu Gaudí
Caja España. Obra social. León
Col·legi de les Teresianes
Consorci de la Colònia Güell
Fundació Caixa Catalunya
Institut Municipal de Parcs i Jardins, Barcelona
Institut de Cultura. Barcelona
Museu d'Història de la Ciutat, Barcelona
Obispado de Astorga
Restaurant Casa Calvet
Restaurant Gaudí Garraf
Departament d'Arquitectura de l'Ajuntament de Barcelona